CREATIVE EDUCATION SPORTS SUPERSTARS

artl
ashe

by Charles and Ann Morse

illustrated by
Harold Henriksen

Amecus Street
Mankato, Minnesota 56001

Published by Amecus Street, 123 South Broad Street, P. O. Box 113, Mankato, Minnesota 56001
Copyright © 1974 by Amecus Street. International copyrights reserved in all countries.
No part of this book may be reproduced in any form without written permission from the publisher.
Printed in the United States.
Distributed by Childrens Press, 1224 West Van Buren Street, Chicago, Illinois 60607
Library of Congress Number: 74-954   ISBN: 0-87191-340-2

Cover: Sports Illustrated photo by Lane Stewart © Time, Inc.

Library of Congress Cataloging in Publication Data
Morse, Charles.   Arthur Ashe.   (Superstars)
SUMMARY: Brief biography concentrating on the career of the black tennis star.
1. Ashe, Arthur—Juvenile literature.   [1. Ashe, Arthur.   2. Tennis—Biography]
I. Morse, Ann, joint author.   II. Henriksen, Harold, illus.
GV994.A7M67   796.34'2'0924   [B]   [92]   74-954   ISBN 0-87191-340-2

arthur ashe

Arthur Ashe Jr., the black tennis star, lived right in the middle of Brook Field, a park in Richmond, Virginia. To a young boy, the park was an athletic paradise. There were tennis courts, a swimming pool, baseball diamonds . . . basketball, football, horseshoe. All were right in his backyard. "I thought it was mine," Arthur said later as he talked about the park.

Arthur's family, like most black families, lived in the "colored section" of Richmond. Arthur went to a different school than the white children. And he played in a different playground. Most of the black men found it hard to find anything but second-class jobs. Arthur was lucky. His father had an interesting job. Mr. Ashe was a special police officer in charge of Brook Field. His family lived in a house in the park. Arthur had one brother, Johnny, who was 4 years younger.

Arthur was born July 10, 1943. His mother taught him to read when he was only 4. All Arthur remembers of his mother is an image of her standing in a blue bathrobe by the door of their house in Brook Field. It was the day she was taken to the hospital. Later Arthur's father explained that she was ill and needed an operation. Mrs. Ashe died five days after the operation. She was only 27. For 6-year-old Arthur, everything changed. His days became lonely.

Arthur would sit by the window and watch the activity in his park. It helped him to forget. Arthur watched a tall young man hit a ball against the practice board on the tennis courts. Arthur watched him intently. The tennis player was also alone.

Mr. Ashe worked hard to keep his family together. He found an older woman, Mrs. Berry, and invited her to come and be part of the family. Arthur didn't like a strange person telling him what to do. But Mrs. Berry was as wise as she was old. She knew that Arthur was grieving for his mother. And she gave Arthur lots of time to work out his sorrow. Little by little, Arthur began to see that someone had to tell him what to do. He decided to try to make the best of it.

Meanwhile, Arthur could escape to his back-yard. He spent most of those lonely days down by the swimming pool or in the horseshoe pits or watching the young man practice on the tennis courts.

One day the young man stopped practicing and looked at the little boy who was watching him. He saw that the boy was carrying a tennis racket. It was almost as big as the boy. "My name is Ronald Charity, what's yours?" he asked Arthur. "Arthur Ashe Junior," Arthur replied.

"Do you want me to show you how to hit the ball?" Ronald asked. With that question, Arthur began his tennis career. Ronald Charity was hired by the Richmond Recreational Department to teach at Brook Field each summer. Ronald showed Arthur how to grip the racket for forehand and backhand drives. He was surprised at how quickly Arthur, who was only 7 years old, learned these strokes. Arthur enjoyed learning tennis from Ronald. Arthur also liked Ronald. He was there just when Arthur needed an older brother.

"Someday I'd like to play tennis as well as Ronald Charity," Arthur told his dad. Arthur's father thought this was a worthwhile goal. But he also made sure that Arthur knew his education came before sports.

Mr. Ashe had walked to school on the first day of school with Arthur. The walk took exactly 10 minutes. Arthur's father told him that each day he must be home exactly 10 minutes after school. Arthur could never go anywhere else before coming home. He knew his father meant what he said.

During the next two summers, Arthur had a busy schedule. Every morning Arthur would play baseball from 9 until noon. Then he'd go over to the swimming pool for a dip before lunch. After lunch Arthur had his practice time with Ronald Charity.

At the end of each summer, Brook Field had a tennis tournament. Most of the tournaments in Richmond were only for white kids. The black children really looked forward to the Brook Field tournament. When Arthur was 9, he and Ronald decided he should enter the tournament. Arthur knew that most of the other boys would be older and bigger, but he wanted to try it anyway. He practiced harder than ever.

One day after practice, Arthur rode around the park on his bicycle. As he coasted toward the tennis court fence, his wheel got caught in a rut and Arthur hit the ground. A few minutes later he realized that he couldn't move his head.

Arthur had broken his collarbone. The doctor assured him that he would be all right. But Arthur would have to go to the hospital. Arthur was very disappointed. The tournament was only 3 weeks away and he surely would miss it.

Arthur recovered quickly and left the hospital one week before the tournament. He worked hard to make up lost time. A week later Arthur was ready to play. Arthur beat a boy 3 years older in the finals. Arthur was the Brook Field tennis champion and he had a medal to prove it.

After Arthur won the Brook Field tournament, Ronald knew that he was running out of things to teach him. Soon after, Ronald brought Arthur to Lynchburg, Virginia, to see Dr. Robert Johnson. Next to medicine, Dr. Johnson loved tennis. He built tennis courts in his own yard. He had helped Althea Gibson, the first black woman tennis star, get started. Dr. Johnson was also on the board of the American Tennis Association (ATA). The ATA was formed by blacks and was similar to the United States Lawn Tennis Association (USLTA).

Dr. Johnson often watched the USLTA Interscholastic Championships held in nearby Charlottesville,

Virginia. He was impressed with the tennis being played in this tournament and in 1950 Johnson entered two boys from Lynchburg. As it happened, Dr. Johnson's entries were quickly beaten in Charlottesville. As he watched them lose, Johnson promised himself that he would develop a young black to win that interscholastic championship. Later on, Johnson was to see many of his dreams fulfilled by Arthur Ashe Jr.

Each year Dr. Johnson invited some of the best young black tennis players to live at his house in the summers. They could practice as a squad and go to tournaments together. The young athletes were given room, board, transportation, and tennis instruction. In return, the group would weed his garden, clip rose

bushes, spray the apple trees, and clean the dog yard.

Dr. Johnson told Ronald that if Arthur was willing to work at tennis, he'd like to invite him to come to his home for 2 weeks that summer. Mr. Ashe wasn't sure he wanted Arthur to go. Arthur was just 10 and that seemed too young to be away from home. But after some thought, Mr. Ashe agreed to let Arthur go.

Dr. Johnson's house seemed like a palace to Arthur. It was a large, 2-story house with tennis courts in the front. The courts were laid several feet above the sidewalk. People passing by got a tennis-shoe view of the matches being played.

When Arthur had been in Lynchburg 3 days,

Dr. Johnson decided he was unteachable. Robert, Johnson's son, found that he couldn't teach Arthur anything new. Arthur would argue that it wasn't the way Ronald had taught him. Finally, Mr. Ashe came and talked to Arthur. He explained that it was Ronald who wanted him there. Arthur understood and stayed. His father made it very clear, then, that Arthur should do everything he was told.

Dr. Johnson recalls that Arthur was the worst player that year. But Arthur was the first person out on the courts every day and the last to leave at night. Johnson admired the boy's endurance. Dr. Johnson says of Arthur, "He did what you told him, even if he lost doing it."

When Arthur returned to Richmond for school that year, he could do something he really liked — play baseball. Compared with baseball Arthur felt that tennis was a pretty lonely sport.

Arthur pitched for the grade school baseball team. He did so well that he made the junior high team. And, of course, he made the tennis team. He didn't have to show up for tennis practice. He just came for the matches and won every time. Arthur never failed to show up for baseball practice. He worked hard at it, but almost always sat on the bench during games. Arthur wondered why.

One morning he got the answer. The principal wanted to see him. He told Arthur that he had pitched his last game. Arthur was stunned. The principal told him that he was just too good a tennis player. He belonged in tennis. And to make sure of it, the principal kicked him off the baseball team. That didn't make Arthur too happy about tennis. He felt forced to play it.

Yet Arthur continued to play tennis. He started looking for players who could give him a tough match. One day he wandered over to Grant Park. The tennis courts here were used only by white people. As he stood at the fence watching the players, a park official noticed him. He came up to Arthur and quietly told him he better leave or there'd be trouble. Arthur didn't argue. But it made him angry. It was one time when he really felt the pinch of prejudice.

Arthur began to feel uneasy about entering tournaments in some of the southern states. Dr. Johnson wanted him to enter a tournament in Florida. Arthur wasn't sure it was a good idea. But Mr. Ashe persuaded him to go. Arthur went and played well. No prejudice was shown. But both Arthur and his father knew that Arthur "had kept his place." For a black, that was outside a white world.

During his last 2 summers at Dr. Johnson's house, Arthur stayed on for a month. He was improving so much, his doctor friend entered him in many tournaments. Arthur still remembers the many trips they took in Dr. Johnson's green Buick.

Arthur was winning often on his trips. In 1958, when Arthur was 14, he won the USLTA under-15 championship. The travel and equipment — rackets, clothes, practice balls — Arthur needed were expensive. His father took some part-time jobs to pay for the equipment. When asked why he would do this for Arthur, Mr. Ashe would say that Arthur was out there on the courts doing some good. Arthur knew that if he slacked up, his dad's money would slack up too. Dr. Johnson also spent money on Arthur. As Arthur improved, 3 white businessmen from Richmond began to support his tennis career. Arthur worked to develop his talent. He didn't want to let his backers down.

In July 1959 Arthur turned 16. It was his last summer at Lynchburg. Dr. Johnson said Arthur was getting so good that he could no longer benefit from the instruction at the Johnsons. Arthur had a burning

wish to play in the Mid-Atlantic Championships that summer. It would be a good place to show his "own home town" how far he had come.

Dr. Johnson filed Arthur's entry well in advance. And he telephoned the club in Washington where the tournament was to be held. But it was no use. Johnson was told that Arthur's name had been entered too late. He and Arthur knew that many white boys had entered that tournament long after Arthur had applied. The white boys would be acceptable on the club's courts; a black would not.

The rejection by the Mid-Atlantic Tournament Committee made Arthur very gloomy. He entered the United States Amateur championships at Forest Hills in 1959 and was beaten by Rod Laver of Australia in the first round. The USLTA rated Arthur as the 44th best player in the country in 1959. Not bad for a 16-year-old. Still Arthur wondered if he should go on with tennis.

But the next summer, 1960, was brighter for Arthur. He won the American Negro Championship. There were over 100 entrants. At 17, Arthur was the youngest winner ever. Also that summer, Arthur was allowed to enter the Mid-Atlantic Tournament. He beat the top ranking Mid-Atlantic player in the finals. Arthur was the first black to win such a title. Arthur was glad he kept on with tennis. He said he was learning something many people before him had learned: nothing needs to get you down permanently.

Near the end of the summer, Dr. Johnson called Arthur and told him he had made plans for him to take his senior year in high school in St. Louis. Richard Hudlin, a black teacher and long-time tennis player, invited him to stay at his home for the year. Johnson explained that Arthur would be able to play against many more whites in St. Louis. Arthur would also be able to play all year on indoor courts. It was settled. Arthur wasn't too happy about going. But he made up his mind to make the best of the opportunity.

The Hudlins made things comfortable for Arthur. Dr. Johnson sent a schedule to Mr. Hudlin and he made sure Arthur followed it. Arthur was up early every morning doing push-ups. He went to school until noon. Then he played tennis all afternoon. Every evening he ran a mile.

When the weather got bad, Arthur moved to an indoor court, a new experience for him. Eventually Arthur played well enough on the faster indoor surfaces

to win the National Junior Indoor Championship twice and the Men's Indoor in 1965.

After the year in St. Louis, Arthur was able to play in the USLTA Interscholastic Tournament in Charlottesville. Arthur took the championship, his second national title, and Dr. Johnson had gotten his wish. Finally one of his black students had captured the title that had been so important to him for many years.

Arthur had received a scholarship offer from J. D. Morgan, tennis coach at UCLA, the University of California at Los Angeles. UCLA was well regarded educationally and had one of the strongest tennis programs in the country. Black athletes had also fared well there. Arthur, his family, and his teachers all felt that it was the best place for Arthur to further his career.

At UCLA Arthur had to make his own decisions. He had to make up his own schedule. He knew he had to get good grades and play tennis well. No one was standing over him showing him how. Arthur liked that.

Arthur became the Number 3 player on the UCLA team. The team was strong. Coach Morgan would stand for nothing else. A tough man with a no-nonsense attitude, Morgan became one of the most powerful men in United States collegiate sports. He is now athletic director at UCLA. By September, 1962, Arthur had improved enough to be the second man on the UCLA varsity team.

By the summer of 1963, Arthur was on the move and he gave Wimbledon a try. Arthur was defeated by America's top-ranked player, Chuck McKinley. But the trip did give him experience in traveling and playing abroad. Arthur came home and won the National Clay Court Championship in Chicago.

A big improvement in Arthur's style was noticeable in this tournament. He was no longer just a slam-bang player. Now Arthur's game was showing more imagination. He was using a variety of different shots. Arthur was beginning to realize that the Davis Cup team was not out of the picture for him. All he needed was to keep winning.

At the Eastern Grass Court Championships in Orange, New Jersey, Arthur lost to Gene Scott. Arthur thought he had also lost his chance for the Davis Cup team. However, on the same day Arthur lost to Scott, he was selected for the Davis Cup team. Arthur was told that the news wouldn't appear in the newspapers until the next day. But word of the "first Negro Davis Cupper" spread and reporters surrounded Arthur.

Since Gene Scott, who had just beaten Arthur, was not picked for the Davis Cup team, some reporters wondered if Arthur was chosen because he was black. When Arthur was asked about this, it was one of the few times Arthur ever showed he was angry. "Just check the won and lost records," Arthur snapped at the reporter.

Arthur entered the 1964 season as the 6th-ranked amateur tennis player in the United States. He returned to Wimbledon but lost to Australia's Roy Emerson. But it was good experience for Arthur to play Emerson. As fast as Arthur was, Emerson was faster. So while Arthur lost, he lost to the best. And Arthur's playing didn't go unnoticed at Wimbledon.

Arthur entered the Eastern Grass Court tournament again in 1964. This time he beat Gene Scott. Arthur also beat Clark Graebner, whose record was every bit as good as Arthur's, and won the title. He was playing so well that he was invited to the United States Amateur Championships at Forest Hills, New York.

Arthur didn't win at Forest Hills, but success soon followed. The U.S. Davis Cup team was playing against Australia in Cleveland. Arthur didn't play in the matches. He was, however, awarded the Johnston

Award. Each year this award is given to the Davis Cup player who shows the most courtesy, character, and spirit of cooperation. It made Arthur very happy. When the award was presented to him, he said, "I hope I can prove to be the exception to the rule that 'good guys' always finish last."

At Forest Hills in 1965, Arthur again met Australia's Roy Emerson in the quarterfinals. Arthur appeared cool. He was not letting Emerson ruffle him and that bothered Emerson. Arthur was a hero for 24 hours.

No American had won the championship at Forest Hills since 1955. And it looked as if Arthur could do it. But the next day, playing Spain's Manuel Santana in the semifinals, Arthur had trouble playing Santana's soft, low balls. Arthur lost. Disappointed, he was even more determined to succeed.

Tennis, now, was no longer just a game for Arthur Ashe. It was a whole way of life. Arthur had become used to the publicity. He liked to see his name in the newspapers or hear it on TV. Now he wanted

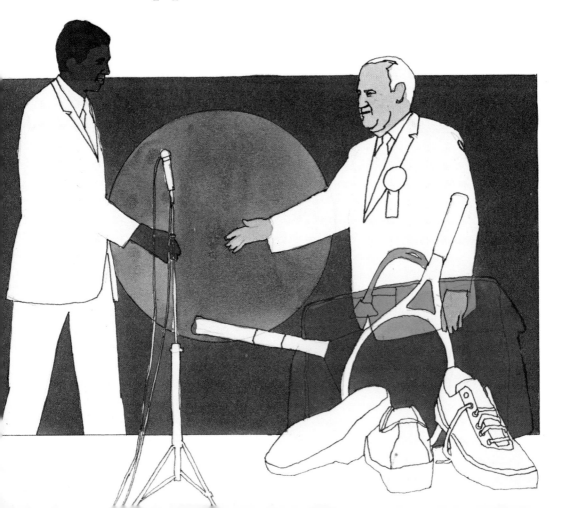

to win one of the Big 4 — the French, Australian, English, and American championships.

During February of 1966, Arthur's senior year at UCLA, he returned to Richmond. The city was celebrating "Arthur Ashe Day." During the ceremonies, Arthur said, "This wouldn't have happened 10 years ago." Everyone dreams about going out and conquering the world, then returning home to claim the honors. Arthur's dream came true.

Arthur graduated from UCLA in June 1966. He was the second-ranked tennis player in the United States.

While in college, Arthur liked fast motorcycles and fast cars. He had long considered music a good friend. Arthur thought of himself as a person who would try almost anything once. He was a fidgety person, always on the go. He would often try to see if he could be the last person to catch a plane.

Instead of parties, Arthur would often go to movies. It was a way for him to lose himself in something different, to forget tennis for a few hours. Arthur says he gets bored easily. His friends in college used to tell him, "Ashe, don't ever get married. You'll be bored with your wife." Arthur may have agreed. At 30, he is still not married.

In February 1967 Arthur became a second lieutenant in the Army. Throughout his 2 years in the Army he continued to play a lot of tennis. The highlight of his tennis career so far came while he was still in the Army. The place was Forest Hills in 1968.

It was the first year Forest Hills was an open tournament — both amateurs and professionals were entered. By the time of the finals in the men's singles, the world's best professionals had been knocked out of competition. Two amateurs were left to play for the first U.S. Open title. They were Tom Okker, a 24-year-old Dutchman, and Arthur Ashe.

The finals were a case of attack and counter-attack. Arthur won a very long first set, 14 games to 12. Okker took the second set 7-5. The third set went to Arthur, 6-3, and it seemed that he would be the winner. But Okker fought back and won the fourth set. In the final set Ashe unleashed his power and ran out the match 6-3. He had just won his first Big 4 title.

It was a thrilling victory for Arthur. He then turned and pointed the handle of his racket to his Davis Cup teammates, bowing to them and giving them a moment of his glory. Arthur was cool. One reporter called it "an air of icy elegance." Then Arthur put his

arm around his weeping father and carried off the silver cup. The first name to be put on the Open cup would be "Arthur Ashe Jr."

As Arthur became an established pro tennis star, he began speaking out more about the problems of blacks in this country and abroad. Once he had felt it was sufficient to set an example. But Arthur is not afraid to change his ideas.

A year after his U.S. Open win, Arthur was refused a visa by South Africa. He had intended to play in that country's championship tournament. South Africa's laws discriminate against blacks. Arthur was refused a visa because he was a black. However, he persisted. Four years later, in November 1973, Arthur became the first black to reach the finals of the South African Open. Here the favored Ashe was upset.

Arthur had been a pro since 1970, the year he won his second Big 4 championship, the Australian Open. The following year he made a good will tour of Africa for the United States government.

Back home at Forest Hills in 1972, Arthur believed he could win again. But Ilie Natase of Rumania beat him in the finals.

In the spring of 1973, Arthur again lost in the

finals of a major event. This time it was the World Championship Tennis Tour.

No one wins all the time in pro tennis. The competition is too good. Losses don't visibly affect Arthur. He always appears relaxed on the courts. He goes for winners. He has been called a master of drop shots. Arthur's greatest weakness seems to be a tendency to hit careless volleys. A volley is a shot hit in the air, often at the net. Arthur will sometimes dump a crucial volley into the cords. Loss of concentration is the enemy of tennis players at all levels. Arthur admits that he sometimes has trouble keeping his mind on his game.

On the court, Arthur's big weapons are his blasting serve and his backhand. Dr. Johnson forced Arthur to work on his backhand. The result is a beautiful, rolling stroke. It is free and open and therefore powerful. Arthur can hit it with underspin, roll it, or hit it flat.

Arthur's backhand is a symbol of the man himself. He took time to develop the stroke, to discipline it. When he hits a backhand in a match, it looks easy. Arthur has also taken the time to develop himself. He is a disciplined person. On and off the court, Arthur appears cool and in command.

JACK NICKLAUS
BILL RUSSELL
MARK SPITZ
VINCE LOMBARDI
BILLIE JEAN KING
ROBERTO CLEMENTE
JOE NAMATH
BOBBY HULL
HANK AARON
JERRY WEST
TOM SEAVER
JACKIE ROBINSON
MUHAMMAD ALI
O. J. SIMPSON
JOHNNY BENCH
WILT CHAMBERLAIN
ARNOLD PALMER
A. J. FOYT
JOHNNY UNITAS
GORDIE HOWE

superstars!
superstars!
superstars
superstars

CREATIVE EDUCATION SPORTS SUPERSTARS

WALT FRAZIER
PHIL AND TONY ESPOSITO
BOB GRIESE
FRANK ROBINSON
PANCHO GONZALES
LEE TREVINO
KAREEM ABDUL JABBAR
JEAN CLAUDE KILLY
EVONNE GOOLAGONG
ARTHUR ASHE
SECRETARIAT
ROGER STAUBACK
FRAN TARKENTON
BOBBY ORR
LARRY CSONKA
BILL WALTON
ALAN PAGE
PEGGY FLEMING
OLGA KORBUT
DON SCHULA
MICKEY MANTLE

R